What Every Child has a Right to Know

By Fr. Thady Doyle

Extra Copies

Extra copies of this booklet can be bought directly from Fr. Thady Doyle, Shillelagh, Arklow, Co. Wicklow, Ireland. The 2010 to 2012 price is €1.50 PLUS postage.

See website www.jesuspowerministries.org for precise price including postage - and also Fr. Thady's other books etc.

Publisher

'What Every Child has a Right to Know' is published by Fr. Thaddeus Doyle, Shillelagh, Arklow, Co. Wicklow, Ireland.

© Fr. Thaddeus Doyle 2010

ISBN 978-0-9560424-3-9

Contents

P. 3 God is love.

P. 5 We will be like Mary.

P. 6 Spirit, Soul and Body.

P. 7 Our Eternal Spirit.

P. 8 Our spirit needs love.

P. 9 Growth of one's spirit.

P. 10 You have a heartroom.

P. 12 Our conscience.

P. 15 Our Will.

P. 16 The eye of the mind.

P. 17 The things that block love.

P. 20 Walking With Jesus.

P. 21 This is true love.

P. 22 Near Death Experiences.

P. 23 When a person who loves God dies.

P. 27 A victim's experience.

P. 32 Baptism in the Spirit.

P. 35 Baptism in the Spirit and Confirmation.

P. 36 When one is hurt.

P. 38 Jesus gives us Himself.

P. 41 Receiving Jesus.

P. 43 The selfish man

P. 46 Finding strength when facing problems

Photos and Images

Cover picture and also the image on P.13

© Copyright Quadriga art, New York used with permission

P. 3, 4, 25 Sunsets by Fr. Liam Kelleher.

P. 36 & 43 Photos by Heart to Hand.

Church windows:- P. 5 Church of Annunciation, Tralee; P. 15, P. 22, P. 41, St. John's Tralee; P. 16 Co. Cork (Buttevant or Charleville); P. 20 Oasis of Peace; P. 21 Callan; P. 35 Duala.

Pictures P. 24, P. 31, P. 37, P. 38, 40, artists are not known to me.
P. 26 Cartoon by Sara Ann Quirke
P. 28 & P. 30, Church banners, artists not known to me. P. 33 cross where Jesus was crucified at Calvary. P. 7 St Therese; P. 12 St. John Vianney; P. 48 Divine Mercy, Andersonstown.

Note concerning the Bible.

I have used a photo of the Good News Bible on P. 14 solely because it has the nicest cover of my various Bibles. My favourite Bible is the RSV, but its language is difficult at times.

Colour consultant: Martina Davis

God Is Love

Here on earth the sun provides the light and the heat. Light and heat shine out from the sun.

In the same way up in Heaven, light and heat shine out from God.

"Heaven does not need the sun or the moon for light as it is lit by the radiant glory of God" Rev 21:23

Light and heat shine out from the Father.

Light and heat shine out from Jesus.

Light and heat shine out from the Holy Spirit.

All the light and heat in Heaven comes from God.

There is so much light and heat coming from God, that Heaven is filled with this most amazing beautiful light and is also lovely and warm.

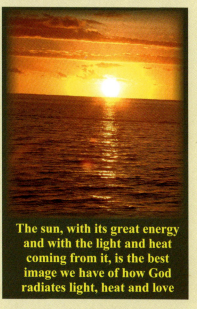

The sun, with its great energy and with the light and heat coming from it, is the best image we have of how God radiates light, heat and love

Just as light and heat radiate out from God, so too love radiates out from God.

On earth we feel the warmth of the light of the sun. When we stand in the sunlight we feel warm.

There is a different type of warmth in the light which comes from God. This light is full of energy and this energy is love.

In the Bible we read, "God energises all things" and "God is love".

Up in Heaven, the saints have an ongoing beautiful experience of an energy embracing them and going right through them that makes them feel loved to the depths of their being.

Just as the energy coming from the sun gives off light and heat, so too the energy that comes from God gives off light, heat and love.

The Father is a real Person who is full of light and full of love, and radiates warmth, and light, and love.

The Risen Jesus is also full of light and full of love, and radiates warmth, and light and love.

The Holy Spirit is also full of light and full of love, and radiates heat, and light and love.

Heaven is full of light, and all that light comes from God:- Father, Son and Holy Spirit.

Heaven is beautifully warm, and all that heat comes from God:- Father, Son, and Holy Spirit.

Heaven is filled with love. Everyone in Heaven has been so embraced in love and so filled with love, that they too radiate love; and all that love comes from God:- Father, Son, and Holy Spirit.

"The Father is love, the Son is love, the Spirit is love. God is wholly and only love" Pope Benedict XV1.

When we die, unless there is something within us to block it, this mighty energy which is love will enter right inside us and make us feel totally and completely loved. **Rejection of God, hatred, and selfishness in its many forms would block God's love from entering into us and filling us with joy when we die.**

Here on earth, a mother will often help her child to feel loved and safe by taking it up, holding it close and cuddling it. When we die, God does the same but in a different way. **Instead of holding us close, His love, unless it is blocked, enters right inside us, lift us up and enables us to feel totally loved to the very depths of our being.**

The good news is that we don't have to wait until we die for that to begin to happen. God desires to begin to pour His love into our hearts right now. Jesus desires to come alive in your heart, to lead you into a living relationship with Himself, and to begin to pour His love into your heart.

So ask Jesus to come alive in your heart and to teach you how to love as He loves.

We Will Be Like Mary

Mary now lives in Heaven, but she has appeared on earth several times. In **Fatima** she appeared to three children, Lucy aged 10, Francisco aged 9 and Jacinta aged 7.

She is now pure spirit, so she can just appear out of nowhere.

In Fatima, one moment she was in front of the children, having appeared out of nowhere. The next moment she was gone again.

She has a body. It is a human body but it is not made from earthly flesh.

This is what we mean when we say that she is now pure spirit. She looks like us, except now she is incredibly beautiful, and there is this amazing light all around her, and one can feel an energy that is love coming out from her.

She has eyes, she has ears, she has a nose, she has a mouth, and she has hands and feet. She also has a heart, and being pure spirit, she was able to allow the children to see her heart beating with love for them.

The Holy Spirit came upon Mary with such power that she conceived Jesus.

She also has a brain, but it is now far more powerful than when she walked the earth. She can now understand things that no one on earth could possibly understand.

While she cannot see the choices that we will make in the future, she can see the difference that these choices will make. She can see how we will bring blessing into the world if we walk with God, and also the hurt that we will cause if we turn our backs on God.

Just like Mary, we too have an eternal spirit that will live on when we die.

Our eternal spirit is already deep within us. It is the most important part of who we are.

Spirit, Soul and Body

Many people say we have a soul as well as a body. This is true, but it does not tell the full story. In the Bible they knew that the human person was far more complex than just body and soul. Thus Mary prayed,

"My soul glorifies the Lord,
My spirit rejoices in God my saviour."

In Hebrews 4:13, we read that the Word of God (The Bible) has the power to reach right in to where the spirit is joined to the soul.

But when they were writing the Bible 2,000 years ago, they were not able to properly explain how the spirit, the soul and the body fitted together.

The Greek wise men believed that we are composed of just two elements:- body and soul. The Greeks were able to explain their beliefs very well, and so their understanding of the human person, that we are just body and soul, came to be accepted by all.

The big weakness in their understanding of the human person is that it does not explain how what we call the soul now lives within the body, and how it interacts with the body and is affected by how we live.

Fr. Tomislav Ivancic gives us a very good explanation of how our eternal spirit, (what the Greeks called the soul), is conjoined to our body.

When Fr. Tomislav was a young man, he got cancer. **When he was only 28, the doctors gave him just two months to live.** Then he was healed during a spiritual experience. That was forty years ago. This experience gave him a great insight into the human person, and into how our eternal spirit, (often called the soul), is conjoined to our mortal body.

He explains that we are composed of three elements

1. An eternal spirit that will live forever.
2. A physical body that will die.
3. What he calls the spiritual soul. This enables our eternal spirit to live in and operate through our physical body

Our Eternal Spirit

Our spirit is the most important element of who we are. Our spirit will live on when our body dies.

We now see through our eyes, yet when we die we will be able to see even better without our present physical eyes. We will still have eyes, but they will not be made from earthly material. They will look like our present eyes but yet they will be different. They will not be made from flesh.

Here on earth we hear with our ears, yet when we die, we will be able to hear even better without our present physical ears. We will have new ears not made from flesh.

We think with our brain, but when we die, we will still be able to think. We will still be able to ask questions and to learn.

Here on earth our eternal spirit is deep within us. It sees through our physical eyes, hears with our physical ears, and thinks with our brain. But when our body dies, we will be able to see even better, hear ever better and think even better.

St Theresa promised to spend her time in Heaven doing good on earth.

If we have lived a loving life on earth, we will still be able to love and be loved, and also to grow in love when we die.

However, if are selfish while on earth, we will still be selfish when we begin life on the other side. If that happens, we will start life on the other side cut off from God's love, and we will find ourselves in a very dark place until our selfishness is dealt with.

If however we invite Jesus into our life and learn to love here on earth, then we will go to Heaven. It is God's desire that we will be able to go straight to Heaven the moment we die - and we will go straight to Heaven if Jesus is truly living in our hearts and we are living by His teaching.

Our eternal spirit that will live on when we die is even now within us. It is the centre of our being.

Our Spirit Needs Love

Just as our lungs need clean air, so too our spirit needs love:- to be loved and to learn to love, if it is to grow and develop properly.

A baby, if starved of love, may even die because its inner spirit is not being nourished.

Many years ago, when the standards of care were much poorer, many babies died in orphanages. **It was discovered that in one orphanage, far fewer babies were dying than in the others.** An investigation was carried out to see what was different in this orphanage. At first, the investigators could find no difference.

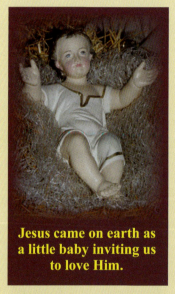

Jesus came on earth as a little baby inviting us to love Him.

Then they discovered that an old woman called Anna was coming into this orphanage, and if any baby wasn't thriving, she took it up and cuddled it. This was the reason that far fewer babies were dying in this orphanage. They were receiving love and this love was nourishing their spirit. With their spirit nourished, they then had the will to live.

Human love comes from the outside. The baby receives the love by being cuddled and cared for, and by hearing love filled words.

God's love comes in a different way to human love.

It comes to us deep inside us. Jesus desires to come alive in our hearts; that is in our eternal spirit at the centre of one's being.

When Jesus comes alive in one's heart (eternal spirit), then He can begin to pour His love right into the centre of one's being.

Even where one did not receive much love as a child, or even if one was hurt, abused or rejected, once Jesus comes alive in one's heart, then He can begin to pour His love into one's heart and to lead one into enormous healing.

Growth Of One's Spirit

First one receives love. Then, for one's spirit to continue to develop, one must learn to give love, to bring love to others.

Real love is prepared to make sacrifices for the good of the person one loves. **A perfect example of real love can be seen in the care of a good parent for a sickly child.** Sometimes a loving parent will have to get up several times every night to comfort a sickly child. This can sometimes go on for several years.

The lack of sleep has a negative impact on the parent's body. One comes to feel like a zombie. One's head feels continuously tired and is easily irritated. One's eyes may become watery, and one may feel a nervous wreck.

But if the parent continues to care for the child with a real desire to surround him or her in love, and without resentment at losing so much sleep, then deep within, his or her inner spirit is growing.

Self-giving love enables one's spirit to grow.

Selfishness, however, destroys one's inner spirit.

Selfishness has the same impact on one's inner spirit that smoking 100 cigarettes a day has on the smoker's lungs.

While acting out of selfless love may sometimes be very hard for the body, as we can see with the parent who loses sleep, yet it is good for the spirit.

Being selfish may sometimes feel very good to the body, but when one is selfish, deep down one's spirit is suffering.

The Dead Sea

One can almost sit on it, but it is the deadest place on earth. Nothing can grow or live in it, so it has no fish and no plants or seaweed. It is full of salt.

The reason for this is that while water flows into it, no water flows out of it.

The spirit of a selfish person is like the Dead Sea. They may receive love, but they do not give it.

Their spirit no longer gives life.

You Have A Heartroom

One's spirit is joined to one's body through a whole series of inner components and cells. These cells and components exist in two main areas of our bodies:- in our brain and in the area within our chest that we often call 'the heart'.

What we call 'the heart' is not the heart that beats and sends blood through one's body. It is that special place deep within us where we feel feelings.

Put your hands to your chest like in the image alongside. Then follow the instructions beneath the image, and see if you can find where the deepest level of the "I" is within you.

That is what we call **"the heart"**. The heart is also sometimes called the centre of our being.

It is also sometimes called our 'personhood'.

It is also the special place where Jesus desires to live within you.

Jesus can really come alive in your heart. He came alive in my heart in a very special way forty years ago. Ever since then, I have had this beautiful experience of Jesus living in my heart. It has changed my whole life.

Jesus loves you every bit as much as He loves me. **Jesus desires to come alive in your heart too.**

Deep within our heart, we also have a special control centre. In God's plan, this control centre

Find Your Heartroom

Place your hands to your chest. Breathe in. Feel the air going into your lungs.

Now think of the person or thing you love most in all the world. Say "I love ..."

Keep repeating "I love ..." until you can feel where the "I" is coming from deep in your chest.

That is the place we call "the heartroom".

It is the centre of our being.

It is where our eternal spirit is conjoined to our body.

It is where you feel empty when lonely, but 'full' if Jesus has come alive in your heart.

deep within our heart, working very closely with our intellect, guides our life.

Our intellect supplies the information and analyses it for us. Our control centre deep within our heart, directs us in how to respond. It gives the basic direction to our life. Again this is the deepest level of the "I" within us.

We were designed by God. God, while three persons, is a mighty energy force of love. It is natural then that, when designing us, He built the need for love and the capacity to love into the very centre of our being.

Our hearts are made to love and be loved.

That is why love is the greatest commandment. Jesus said, **"You shall love the Lord your God with all your mind, with all your heart and with all your soul. .... You shall love your neighbour as yourself."** The only way to become open to God who is love, is by learning to love.

The Heart of Jesus

Just as our heart is the very centre of our being, so too the heart of Jesus is the centre of His being. **Jesus is love, so His heart is a mighty energy force of love.** He loves us from the depths of His heart.

Sometimes when Jesus appeared to saints, like **St. Margaret Mary**, He showed them His heart filled with love for us.

He invites us to pray to His Sacred Heart.

Many people, when they have a special intention, repeat the following prayer nine times,

May your Sacred Heart, Lord Jesus, be praised, glorified and honoured throughout the whole world now and forever more.

As you pray that prayer, form a mental picture of blessing going out from the heart of Jesus to embrace your special intention.

Praying to His Sacred Heart opens us to His great love, and releases blessing into the world. **As a result we will often see our prayers answered.**

Our Conscience

One's brain is the other key area where one's eternal spirit is conjoined to one's mortal body.

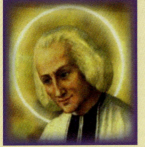

The most important part of the brain is the intellect. We use our intellect all the time. You are using it right now as you read this booklet.

Our intellect takes in all the information we receive, analyses it, stores it and suggests ways in which this information can be used and how best to respond to it.

An Example

If you hear that there is about to be a big storm, your intellect takes in this information. It thinks of what the risks are, and comes up with ideas as to how to respond. This information is then fed to the control centre deep in your being, the depths of the "I" within you. Your control centre then takes control of your response, assisted by your will.

Our conscience is part of our intellect.

The function of our conscience is to help us to know what is right before God. We have many choices to make in life. Indeed every day we are making choices. God gave us a conscience to help us to make the right choices.

Many people confuse their conscience with their feelings. They think that if something 'feels' right, that then it is right for them. But feelings spring from the area that we call the heart. The conscience is located in the brain, and has its own special brain cells within the intellect.

When trying to decide if something is the right thing to do, the first question one should ask oneself is, not does this feel good, but is this right before God?

The purpose of conscience is to help us to see what is right in the eyes of God.

To be able to know what is right before God, we need to know what God actually teaches us. To help us to know what is right God gave Moses the

10 commandments. The 10 commandments are a set of basic rules.

Then, when Jesus came on earth, He taught us how to live as a child of God who is love.

God is love. Jesus is love. So all the teaching of Jesus centres on love.

Jesus explained that the first and greatest commandment is, **"You shall love the Lord your God with all your mind, with all your heart, with all your soul, and with all your strength."**

Why is that the most important commandment?

Because God is love, and when we respond to Him with love, then He can begin to pour His love into our hearts.

Jesus told his followers that He was giving them a new commandment:- **"Love one another as I have loved you."**

This is the new commandment because, since God is love, His followers are called to centre their lives on love.

Jesus also taught us how to love. **He loved us so much that He gave His life for us.** That is true love.

Jesus also said, **"Blessed are the peacemakers because they shall be called children of God"** (Matthew 5:9).

Why are peacemakers children of God? Because God is love.

He also said, **"Love your enemies and pray for those who persecute you and then you will be sons and daughters of the Father who makes his sun shine on good and bad men alike"** (Matthew 5:44)

Why are those who love their enemies sons and daughters of the Father? Because God is love.

Jesus was speaking here to adults. When a child is being being bullied or in some way abused, the child should immediately seek the help of an adult. **Jesus does not expect a child who is being bullied or abused to** be able to love the offender without first getting help from adults.

He also told those who hurt children that it would be better for them to have a great millstone tied around their necks and to be dumped in the sea. He gave adults this warning, because when we hurt others, it cuts us off from God's love. **It is a terrible thing to die while cut off from God's love.**

Jesus also gave us much more teaching about how we are to live. We find this in the Bible.

The Bible contains two main sections. The larger part is known as the **Old Testament**. It was written before the time of Jesus. There are many wonderful passages in the Old Testament. But they hadn't yet come to know that God is love . Sometimes they believed that God is vengeful and that He zapped his enemies. **As a result, the Old Testament, as the Catholic Church teaches, contains some elements that are imperfect.**

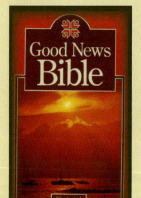

The **New Testament** is far shorter than the Old Testament. It contains the teaching of Jesus, and also teaching by St. Paul, St. Peter and St. John.

It is very good practice to read a passage of the New Testament every day.

Jesus can really speak to us through the Bible - especially at important moments in our lives when we have big decisions to make.

The Church also assists us in how to apply the teaching of Jesus and the Bible to the situations we face in daily living.

All this information is a great help to our conscience as it seeks to guide us in what is right. But our conscience is also influenced by what is in our hearts.

Our conscience can only recognise what is right before God, if in our heart, we desire to do what is right before God.

If in our heart we have rejected God, or become selfish, or allowed greed, or hatred, or jealousy or any other negative power control in our heart, then it will be almost impossible for our conscience to guide us.

Our Will

Another very important part of one's brain is one's will. It too has its own special brain cells. It is that part of the brain that gives us the mental strength to do what we desire to do.

If one makes a habit of doing what is right, one builds up strength in one's will. One then has what is known as "free will". Then one is able to freely do what is right.

One's heart desires to do what is right.

One's conscience is able to show one what is right.

One's will is able to see to it that one does what is right.

But if one makes selfish choices, one's will loses its strength.

A time comes when, even if one desires to do what is right, one hasn't the 'will power' to do it. Then one no longer has 'free' will, for one's will has lost its ability to act freely. It has become enslaved to one's own selfish desires.

Then we say that the person has a compulsion to act in this way. The will no longer has the strength to do what is right. Even if one decides to do what is right, one falls back into the same old weakness. One is then a slave to one's desires.

One could become a slave to drink, or to drugs, or to anger, or to worrying, or to fears, or to greed, or to jealousy or to any number of other things. Once one becomes a slave, one may no longer be able to free oneself.

These compulsions can however be broken by learning to depend on God's power.

Some people call God's power the **"Higher Power"**. There are special programmes, often called 12 step programmes, that are designed to help people to break free of their compulsions, by learning to depend on God's power. For example, the 12 step programme for people who are addicted to alcohol is operated by a group known as Alcoholics Anonymous.

The Eye Of The Mind

Another special spiritual gift, with its own special brain cells, is the ability to mentally picture things. We use this gift when we draw and paint, and when we design or invent things.

A very special use of this gift is to mentally picture Jesus going before us and to then draw strength from Him.

Jesus is with you right at this moment, but you cannot see Him with your physical eyes. You can however 'see Him' with what is sometimes called **the eye of the mind**.

Think of someone you love. Form a picture of them in your mind.

Now form a mental picture of Jesus.

Jesus promised to go before us always. It can be a great help, especially if one is nervous, to have a mental picture of Jesus going before you, giving you strength for every situation.

In your prayer time, this could be a fairly clear mental picture of Jesus.

But when speaking, it is best that this be just a mere glimpse in your mind's eye of Jesus going before you, offering you strength.

I once found it very hard to speak in public. So, when I had to do so, I allowed a very vague mental picture of Jesus into my mind. I pictured Jesus being before me giving me strength.

As long as I kept my eye on Jesus, I could forget my nervousness and speak effectively. **Mentally picturing Jesus in this way has helped countless people.** Jesus is with us always. He desires to give us strength. Our physical eyes cannot see Him. But the eye of the mind allows our inner spirit to see Him and to draw strength from Him.

"I saw the Lord before me always,
for with Him at my right hand nothing can shake me.
Then my heart was glad and my spirit rejoiced" Acts 2:25

Things That Block Love

God is love, totally and completely love. Our eternal spirit is specially designed by God to love and to be loved.

Our spiritual soul that enables our eternal spirit to live in union with our mortal bodies is also designed for love; to love and to be loved.

So the entire centre of our being is designed for love:- to be loved and to become a centre of love, bringing love to others.

But sometimes hurt, bitterness, selfishness or fear can enter our hearts. These block love. What do we need to do then to become open to God who is love?

Suppose one has a jam jar filled with dirty water. What would we need to do to fill the jar with air?

1. Recognise that the dirty water is blocking the air from coming in.
2. Unscrew the cap
3. Empty out the dirty water.

Air and dirty water do not mix. Once the dirty water has been emptied out, the air will freely come into the jar.

So too with God's love in our hearts. God absolutely loves you. He desires to pour His love into your heart.

But just as air and dirty water cannot mix, so too there are certain things that love cannot mix with.

Love and selfishness cannot mix.
Love and greed cannot mix.
Love and hatred cannot mix.
Love and bitterness cannot mix.
Love and resentfulness cannot mix.
Love and bullying cannot mix
Love and abusiveness cannot mix.
Love and self-pity cannot mix.
Love and jealousy cannot mix.
Love and cheating or stealing cannot mix.

Love and vandalism cannot mix.
Love and judgementalism cannot mix.
Love and prejudice cannot mix.
Love and using others cannot mix.
Love and pride cannot mix.
Love and vulgarity cannot mix.
Love and self-indulgence cannot mix.
Love and selfish ambition cannot mix.
Love and impatience cannot mix.
Love and meanness cannot mix.
Love and fear cannot mix.

If any of these things are in our hearts, they block the flow of God's love. God still loves us. If we ask Him, Jesus will still live in our hearts, but His love cannot flow through our hearts.

Just as the moon cuts off the sun's light during an eclipse, so too sin blocks God's love from entering one's spirit.

Not merely do they block the flow of God's love in our hearts, but they cause damage to our inner being, to that part of our inner selves where our eternal spirit is conjoined to our mortal bodies. Our eternal spirit and our inner being are both made to love and be loved. If we allow any of these other things to get a grip on us, there is real damage being done to both our eternal spirit and our spiritual soul where our eternal spirit joins our mortal bodies.

Worse still, if we die with any of these things embedded in our spirit, they will block God's love.

It will be like an eclipse of the sun. We will find ourselves in a place of darkness and desolation. Then we will have to go through a painful process of facing the truth about the hurt we have caused here on earth, crying out to God, and being cleansed of everything that blocks love.

What do we need to do to be cleansed now?

Just like with emptying out the dirty water, there are three steps to take.

1. Identify anything in your heart that blocks love. As a help to this go through the list of things on pages 17-18 that cannot mix with love. See if any of these negative things are in your mind or heart.

2. **Unscrew the lid to your heart.** The way to unscrew the lid to our hearts is by desiring to have our hearts cleansed. We have been given free will. Jesus will never force us to cleanse our hearts of the things that block love. Having first identified anything in your heart that blocks love, desire to be set free of it.

3. **Empty out.** Emptying the dirty water from the jar was easy. It is not nearly so easy to empty out from our hearts the things that block love. If they have got deeply ingrained in one's heart, one will need help.

One very special help that Jesus has given us for this process is the Sacrament of Confession.

Alcoholics Anonymous is a very special programme to help alcoholics break their addiction to alcohol. They have a 12 step programme which enables the alcoholic to break from his or her addiction.

These steps include

Step 4. Made a searching and fearless moral inventory of ourselves. (We call that making a good examination of one's conscience.)

Step 5. Admitted to God, to ourselves, and to another human being, the exact nature of our wrongs.

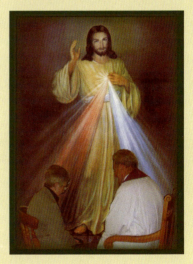

We can take these exact same steps in Confession.

The Sacrament of Confession will become a real sacrament of healing for us if we do the following three things,

1. Make a decision that will be totally honest with the priest.

2. Find some priest that we can go to Confession to face to face.

3. Go to the same priest on a regular basis - perhaps once a month.

Take these three steps and the Sacrament of Confession will open you to the light of Christ, and it will become a source of ongoing healing in your life.

Walking With Jesus

Many people just get up every morning and rush into the day. They may have plans about how to make money, or about how to do something or to achieve something, but that is all. Some sadly make the world a worse place in which to live and bring hurt into the lives of others.

True children of God desire to make the world a better place.

Today Jesus has no hands but ours, and no way of entering the world but through our hearts.

His true children welcome Him to live in their hearts, and then seek to become His hands and His voice in today's world.

They desire to live in such deep union with God who is love, that they will be bearers of love and blessing to every person they meet.

The true child of God will make the world a better place each day just by being alive.

Living in union with Jesus who is love, the true child of God becomes a living radiator of love and goodness.

Today Jesus has no hands but ours, no feet but ours, no voice but ours.

Sometimes one will still make mistakes, possibly causing hurt to others. Then one will turn to God who is Love and accept His forgiveness.

Then renewed by God's love, instead of beating oneself up, one will seek to heal the hurt that one has caused, and also seek to do better in future.

Some Special Prayers

Lord Jesus, I welcome You to live within me.
Come alive in my heart today.

May Your love be so poured into my heart that it will begin to shine out through my eyes and be reflected in my speech.

Help me to make the world a better place
and to bring blessing into the life of some person this very day.

This Is True Love

Jesus came on earth out of love for us.

He lived a life of deep love for His Father.

He sought to reach out to every person He met with love.

He freely gave His life out of love for us.

Right up to the last, He could have avoided being crucified. He knew that if He went to Jerusalem, that He would be crucified, yet He still went.

Even after He was arrested, He could have avoided crucifixion by denying His mission.

But He loved His Father and He wanted to do His will in all things.

He also loved us. He knew that selfishness, greed, and anger had entered the human heart. **He knew that we could only be saved by a total act of love.** And so out of love for us, He gave Himself up to a truly horrible death.

In doing so, He won for us the right to eternal life. He can now come alive in our hearts, cleanse us from sin, begin to pour His love into our hearts, and lead us into God's special plan for our lives.

He has also shown us what TRUE love really is.

Some people speak of being in love, but the only person they really love or are thinking about, is themselves.

TRUE love is prepared to give of oneself even when it is costly or painful to do so.

TRUE love will put the good of the person one loves before oneself.

TRUE love will never use another person.

TRUE love will never try to control or to possess another person.

TRUE love will always want the best for the person that one loves.

Near Death Experiences

Lazarus had already been in the tomb for four days when Jesus raised him from the dead. Did you ever wonder where Lazarus's spirit was during those four days?

In recent years there have been some remarkable stories of people coming back to life after being declared dead. Take the case of George Rodonaia.

He was assassinated by the KGB. A car drove straight into him at speed, then reversed and drove over him again. He was declared dead. His mangled body was taken to the mortuary, the special place where dead bodies are taken.

It was then placed in the refrigerator unit of the mortuary and left there for three days. Then it was taken back out for the autopsy. **But just as his body was being cut into for the autopsy, George came back to life.**

You can guess the shock that the doctor got when the dead man on the slab came back to life. You can also guess how cold George felt after his body had been left for three days in the refrigerator unit of the mortuary.

George had a remarkable story to tell of what he experienced on the other side, and of how he met Jesus there.

Before his experience George had been an atheist, that is he did not believe in God. After his experience, not merely did he believe in God, but he became a priest in the Russian Orthodox Church.

Many people, just like George, have had what are called "near death experiences". Some claim to have learned all sorts of things while their spirit was outside their body. But there is a different way of learning when our spirit leaves our body. The answers to one's questions just come into one's mind. The problem is that if one's spirit is not fully tuned in to God, the answer that comes into one's mind could be totally wrong.

So one has to be careful with what people claim to have learned during their near death experiences, but near death experiences are very real. They do happen. **We do have an eternal spirit that lives on.**

When a person who loves God dies

Don Piper is a really good man. He loves God. He loves his wife and loves his children. Jesus is truly his best Friend.

One weekend he went to a big Christian gathering to learn more about Jesus. A terrible storm set in, so they were sent home early. As Don drove home in his car, he had to cross a long narrow bridge.

Suddenly a big juggernaut came from the opposite direction. It was going too fast. The driver lost control, and crashed head-on into Don's car. Not merely did it crash into Don's car, but it jumped up onto his car and went right over it, all eight wheels of one side of the juggernaut going over his car, crushing the car and crushing Don inside it.

We need to pray for God's protection when on the roads

A doctor arrived on the scene within minutes. He examined Don. There were massive injuries. There was blood coming from his eyes, ears, nose and mouth. His body was all mangled. **The doctor examined him and declared him dead**. He said that he had been killed instantly.

A cover was placed over the car. Because he was dead, the plan was for his body to be taken, not to a hospital, but to the mortuary, that is the special place where dead people's bodies are kept. But before his body could be taken to the mortuary, he had to be declared dead by a senior doctor. **The senior doctor arrived on the scene of the accident about an hour later. He examined Don's body and he too declared him dead.**

Meanwhile the road was blocked. Traffic backed up for miles in both directions. A Baptist minister called Dick, who was a friend of Don's, was stuck way back in the blocked traffic. He walked up to the scene of the accident, and asked the policeman if there was anybody he could help. The policeman suggested that he speak to a couple of people whose car had been slightly damaged as the juggernaut came to a halt. They were not injured, but they were in shock. **However Dick began to feel that God was asking him to pray for the dead man.**

So he went over to the covered over car. The juggernaut had torn off the back of the car, what is called the hatchback, so even though the car was crushed, Dick was able to crawl in from the back. He managed to squeeze his way up to where Don's body was lying mangled and crushed.

Dick had trained as a junior doctor before he became a Baptist minister. So the first thing he did was to check for signs of life. There were none. **Don was still dead.**

Dick started to pray over him. After praying for several minutes, Dick started to gently sing the beautiful hymn, **"What a friend we have in Jesus".**

Guess his surprise when the 'dead' man started to sing it with him!

Dick crawled back out of the car as fast as he could, and went running over to the ambulance driver and nurses, shouting out, **"He is not dead. He is alive."**

Don had been examined and declared dead by two doctors. Indeed anyone who saw him, saw that he was clearly dead. Yet here was Dick claiming that Don was alive. **They thought that Dick was a nut case.**

Dick was very excited, and finding himself not being believed, he started shouting, **"He is not dead. He is singing."**

You can guess their reaction when he starting shouting that the dead man was singing. They really thought that he was imagining things. So Dick threatened to lie down on the road in front of the ambulance if they didn't examine Don. They still thought that Dick was nuts, but to keep him happy, the medic went over and had a look at Don. What a surprise he got when he discovered that Don was now alive.

They had to wait a further half hour for cutting equipment to come to cut Don out of the car. Eventually Don was taken to hospital, and began a very long process of treatment for his massive injuries. As a matter of interest, a section of bone from one of his legs was never found, and also a section of bone from one of his arms was never found. He would have bled to death had he been alive during the hour and a half that he was left for dead.

He came back alive singing **"What a friend we have in Jesus"**.

If we were to experience what Don claims to have experienced during those ninety minutes that he was at the gates of Heaven, we too would be singing "What a friend we have in Jesus".

Remember that Don was a really good man. He loved God. He loved his wife. He was a wonderful father to his children. **He was ready to go straight to Heaven the moment he died.** So the very moment he 'died' he went straight to the gates of Heaven.

God is love. God absolutely completely and totally is love. On earth it is the sun that gives us both light and heat. **Up in Heaven, it is God who gives both the light and the heat; and the light and heat coming from God are filled with love.**

Everyone in Heaven is full of love. Love just shines out from them.

For ninety minutes Don was at the very entrance to Heaven, and his description of what he experienced there is very special.

First there was this beautiful light. While Don didn't see God, he knew that this beautiful light came from God Himself and it was full of love. **Don never experienced light like it on earth.** Not merely did it completely light up the place, but it gave off a lovely warm feeling and made one feel totally loved. **At the entrance to Heaven, Don experienced a happiness that he never believed to be possible.**

Secondly all the people who had died who had helped him on earth, formed a welcoming party to meet him at the gates of Heaven. **They too were so full of love that it was shining out through them.** He says it was the most wonderful family reunion that he was ever at.

When Don was a little boy, his closest friend had been killed in a tragic road accident. At the time, Don was really upset. He was only a little boy back then. His heart was just full of grief when his best friend was killed, and some of that grief had stayed in his heart all his life.

But now amongst those there waiting to greet him at the gates of Heaven was his childhood friend Mike. **Like all the others, the love was just shining out of Mike's eyes, and now, at last, Don felt all the grief leaving his heart.**

Also waiting to greet him was his grandmother. She had been a native American, what some people call an Indian. **She had had a very tough life, and died while Don was still very young.** All he remembered of her was this little old woman, who was all bent over as she walked, her face completely wrinkled, and without a tooth in her mouth, because while she had false teeth (dentures), they were seldom in her mouth.

Now here she was, standing completely upright, her face radiating love, and with the most perfect set of teeth in her mouth that were clearly her own.

Thirdly there was the music and singing. Don had never heard anything nearly so beautiful. It was the same as if every hymn he had ever heard was being sung together in perfect harmony with the most beautiful backing music which he believes to have been provided by the angels.

And Don was just at the gates of Heaven. Imagine what it must be like in Heaven itself.

Suggested Exercise

Get your parents to tell you about the people in your family who are now dead, who truly loved God and loved other people. If they loved God and loved others, they are now either in Heaven or in the upper levels of Purgatory where people are so happy that they sometimes think that they are in Heaven. These are part of your family. You can look forward to meeting them when you go to Heaven. Ask your parents to tell you about them and to show you their photographs.

Then ask your parents to tell you if any member of your family who has died, might still need your prayers because of the way they lived.

A Victim's Experience

When Barbara Harris Whitfield was a little child, her mother was a very sick woman mentally and emotionally.

Barbara's father wasn't able to cope with his wife's continuous fighting, so he stayed out of the house as much as possible. But that left little Barbara alone with her mother. **Her mother was continuously shouting at her, calling her bad names and telling her that she was no good.**

Her mother was also continuously going to doctors. It wasn't that she was really sick. Going to doctors was her way of getting attention.

She had a whole wardrobe full of beautiful shoes. All these shoes were very tight fitting, as she desired for her feet to appear small and dainty. But then her feet grew a little bit or became enlarged. As a result, her shoes started to really hurt her. She kept complaining to her doctor about this problem.

Eventually he said to her, "Look woman you have a choice. You can either get new shoes or you can get your toes shortened."

Guess which she did! She got her toes shortened! This was just one of 25 'elective' operations that she had while Barbara was growing up.

When Barbara was a child, she prayed hard that God would send a doctor who would be able to cure her mother.

But instead of seeing her mother cured, she saw her going back into hospital again and again. When her mother was in hospital, Barbara would feel very alone as she had no friends. Then her mother would come home and start shouting at her and abusing her all over again.

So when her mother was in hospital, Barbara was sad and lonely, and when her mother was at home, Barbara was hurt and upset by what her mother said to her. **It was a terrible life for little Barbara.** It was more than any child could cope with. To be able to survive, Barbara started to blot out her feelings. This is sometimes called psychic numbing.

She also lost belief in God. Given that her mother was so cruel to her, and that her father was never there for her, it was easier for her to believe that there was no God, than to believe that there is a God and that He was ignoring her prayers and didn't love her.

When Barbara grew up, she had to go into hospital for a major operation on her back, due to her having severe curvature of her spine. It was a major operation. Shortly after the operation, a bad infection set in and she ended up on death's door. **Then she had a near death experience.** Her eternal spirit left her body and she found herself looking down on her body in the bed down below. **Then, while still outside her body, she met her grandmother who had died some years previously.**

Her grandmother was the one person who had ever really loved her. God, who is love, now allowed Barbara to re-experience every precious moment that she had ever spent with her grandmother. She found herself back as a little child in her grandmother's house, with her grandmother allowing her to help with the mixing of the materials for the baking of bread, and then her grandmother holding her close, caressing her and combing her hair.

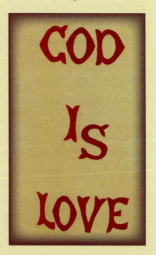

God, who is love, allowed her to relive every precious moment of love she had ever spent with her grandmother. This is something that God often does, during their near death experiences, for people who feel sad because of all the hurt they have suffered.

Sometimes people who have been hurt a lot, come to think that nobody ever loved them. **It is so much easier to remember all the bad things that happen to us, than to remember the love we have been given.**

When people who have suffered a lot of hurt have near death experiences, God, who is love, allows them to re-experience every moment of love they ever experienced. Being allowed to re-experience the times when they were loved, helps them to become open to God's love and to healing.

It can be very helpful for us too to relive in our minds and hearts all the moments of love and happiness that we have experienced.

After being allowed to relive every precious moment she had experienced with her grandmother, Barbara came back into her body. She told the nurses what she had experienced, but they tried to tell her that it was all only her imagination. They told her that it was merely chemical reactions in the brain when one is close to death.

Some days later she suffered an even more severe relapse with the infection. Once again she 'died', that is her eternal spirit left her body.

This time she found herself being lifted up by a mighty energy force that permeated her to the very depths of her being and made her feel totally and completely loved.

She found her entire inner self being embraced by an energy that gave her a sense of being loved that she never thought possible.

It lifted her up. It went right through her. It made her feel warm and happy, and gave her this incredible feeling of being loved.

She just knew that she was being embraced by God; that God had actually come inside her and was filling her with His love.

But she didn't see God. She thinks that it wasn't the Christian God she met, because she thinks that if it was the Christian God, she should have seen a person. It is indeed true that when people meet Jesus or the Father on the other side, they see a God in the form of a human being.

But there is also the Holy Spirit. The Holy Spirit does not appear in human form. **It was the Holy Spirit that Barbara experienced.** Sadly to this day she does not know this.

As she was being lifted up in this mighty energy that she knew to be God, and that permeated her to the depths of her being, and made her feel loved in a way she had never before experienced, she was allowed to relive her entire past including all the times her mother had abused her. But this time, as she was reliving it, she was being held aloft by Love, with love filling her entire inner being, making her feel totally secure.

This time also she was able to feel the feelings. When the abuse had happened to her as a child, the only way she could cope was by blotting out her feelings. That is a way of coping that doctors call psychic numbing. One numbs one's feelings in order to survive. This causes a lot of damage deep within, and before real healing can take place, one must learn to feel the feelings of sadness, hurt and upset.

As Barbara relived her painful childhood, while in her inner being she was being permeated by love, in her emotions she could now allow herself to feel the pain of her mother's abuse.

God also allowed Barbara to see that her mother was a sick woman, and to see how her mother had herself been hurt as a child.

Her mother had been badly mistreated by her own father, and this led to her becoming the sick person that she now was.

Some people, who set out to do good in life, end up making mistakes that cause real hurt to others either as a result of being hurt themselves, or through the pressures of life. Barbara's mother was one of those. **As God allowed her to see this, Barbara was able to forgive her mother for all the hurt that she had caused her.**

God also allowed Barbara to see that, when as a child she had prayed for her mother to be healed, it wasn't that God hadn't heard her prayers, but rather that her mother didn't want to be cured. Her mother's way of getting attention was by being sick. Since being sick got her attention, she became an expert in being sick so as to get attention.

Barbara herself had also made many mistakes in life. Now she was allowed to see these mistakes too, but once again she saw them while being held up by God's mighty love. While she had made mistakes, she wasn't really to blame for them. It was the way that she had been hurt that caused her to make these mistakes. God still loves us even when we make mistakes.

Barbara believes that during this time she was in Heaven. She wasn't. She was in the upper regions of the place we call Purgatory.

Purgatory is a special place of God's mercy for people who are not yet ready for Heaven. People in the upper regions of Purgatory are already open to God's love, so it is a very happy place. Here they learn how to respond to love and to be transformed by love. **Wonderful things happen in the upper regions of Purgatory.** One learns to love just as God loves, and one prays for God to heal and bless anyone that one has hurt.

While it too is a place of God's mercy, the depths of Purgatory are very different. Selfish people, who by God's mercy are saved from going to Hell, go there. There they have to learn to face the truth about their lives, including the truth about how they rejected God, about how selfish they were, and about the hurt that they caused to others.

It can take some of them a long time to face the truth about how they lived, to repent of their sins, and to become open to God's love. At first, until they begin to open their hearts to God, they can suffer great anguish.

But it was in the upper realms of Purgatory that Barbara was. She was so happy there that she thinks that she was in Heaven.

Jesus, Mary, the Holy Spirit and even God the Father visit those in the upper regions of Purgatory.

On her way back to her body, she visited other parts of the hospital - including the nurses station and overheard them talking.

When she came back into her body, the nurses once again tried to tell her that her experience wasn't real, and that it was only all in her imagination. But this time, she was able to tell them what they had been talking about down in the nurses station.

To this day, Barbara does not realise that it was the Holy Spirit she experienced. Because of that, she does not have the benefit of the teaching of the Bible or of the Catholic Church, so she may end up coming up with some very wrong ideas about God and about how to live.

But she knows that God is Love, and that is the most important thing to know about God.

Baptism In The Spirit

Barbara Harris Whitfield was permeated by God's incredible love while outside her body. She had the incredible experience of being lifted up by a mighty energy force that is Love itself (the Holy Spirit), and of this Love filling her heart and enabling her to deal with her very painful past, and then enabling her to live a new life.

It is God's desire that we experience this outpouring of love while still in our mortal bodies. Jesus called this **"Baptism in the Spirit"**. Before going into Heaven, Jesus said to His followers, **"John baptised with water, but within days you will be baptised with the Holy Spirit"** Acts 1:5.

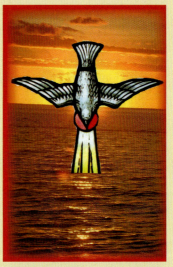

We can best understand what Jesus was promising if we understand how the word baptism was understood in the time of Jesus.

Before John the Baptist, the word 'baptism' wasn't a religious word at all. It simply meant to be dipped in water.

That is why, when John the Baptist started dipping people in the River Jordan, people said that he was baptising them. The reason they said he was baptising them was simply because he was dipping them in the water.

The word 'baptism' also meant to be flooded. If a house or a street was flooded, people said it was baptised.

In the textile industry, clothes were dyed by being dipped down into a big vat of dye. People again said that the clothes were being baptised.

So the word 'baptism' had three meanings:-

To be dipped in water,

To be flooded,

And to be dyed through and through.

Each of these three meanings help us to understand what Jesus meant when He said, "Within days you will be baptised with the Holy Spirit."

To Be Dipped:- In Baptism what is dipped into what?

In the early Church, they had a pool of water beside every Church. On Holy Saturday night, those being baptised went down three steps into the water. Then they were dipped down into it. Then they came up three steps at the other side, where, having been dried, they put on a white garment.

They expected that something very special would happen at the moment they went down into the water.

Firstly they expected that Jesus would come alive in their hearts.

They also believed that they were being united with Jesus at the very moment of his death and resurrection.

Going down the three steps into the water and being dipped in it was a symbol of being united with Jesus in His death. Coming up the three steps out of the water was a symbol of being united with Jesus in His resurrection.

As a result of being united with Jesus at this special moment, they expected the power of Jesus to enter their inner being, and that Jesus coming alive in their hearts, would give them the strength to love in a new way and to break free of sinful habits.

They put on the special white garment as a symbol of the new life they could now live. **So in Baptism, we are not just dipped into the water, but also into the death and resurrection of Jesus.** Read Romans 6:3-5.

By virtue of your Baptism, Jesus is already within you. Invite Him to come alive in your heart, and pray to become open to His love.

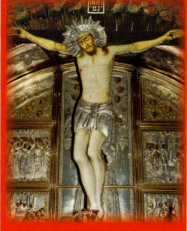

Jesus took our sins with Him to the cross.

What is your greatest weakness or sin? Jesus took that with Him to the cross.

He won for you the right to forgiveness for it.

He also won for you the right to be set free of it.

In Baptism, we are united with Jesus as the special moment of his death and resurrection.

He can now come alive in your heart, and by his power, you can be set free of your sins.

Picture:- The cross that now stands where Jesus was crucified on Calvary.

To Be Flooded

The second meaning of the word 'baptism' was to be flooded.

In Baptism in the Spirit, what needs to be flooded with what?

Our inner heartroom needs to be flooded with the indwelling Jesus, and with a deep sense of being loved by God.

Our heartroom is that special place where our eternal spirit is conjoined to our mortal body. This is where Jesus desires to live. It is a most wonderful experience to have a sense of Jesus coming alive deep within you.

Put your hands to your chest and ask Jesus to pour His love into your heart.

Jesus is love. The Holy Spirit is love. Once Jesus comes alive in your heart, the Holy Spirit can begin to pour love into your heart. To have a personal experience that God is love and that God loves you is another key element of Baptism in the Spirit.

To Be Dyed Right Through

The third original meaning of the word baptism was for a garment to be dyed right through. In Baptism in the Spirit, what needs to be dyed through and through with what?

Just as in the dye trade, the dye goes right through the garment, so too in our case, our entire inner being needs to be penetrated through and through by the healing, cleansing and delivering power of the Holy Spirit.

In some parts of our inner selves, where our inner being has been hurt or damaged, either by the way we have been treated by others or by our own wrong choices, we need healing. Healing is primarily the work of Jesus, but it is also the work of the Holy Spirit.

We also need inner cleansing. Our memories, our conscience, and sometimes our hormones and emotions need cleansing.

If we have compulsive tendencies, big or small, we need deliverance. By learning to depend on Jesus, who is both within us and before us, we can break free of every compulsion. For people with big compulsions, there are special steps to help them become open to this Higher Power.

Baptism in the Spirit and Confirmation

Jesus promised His friends that they would be baptised with the Holy Spirit. He said that this would be different to being baptised with water - though it can take place while a person is being baptised with water.

Baptism in the Spirit is above all about having one's inner spirit flooded with and permeated by God's love.

There are also several other elements to Baptism in the Spirit.

Jesus desires for you to know Him as a real person and for you to have a living relationship with you.

He desires for you to know that He is Love, and that He loves you.

He desires to come alive in your heart in a way that you will actually experience.

He desires to heal you of your inner hurts.

He desires to help you overcome your fears.

He desires you to know that He has a special plan for your life.

He desires for you to come to know Him as your best friend.

He would love for you to start spending real time talking to Him, and for this time to bring strength and peace into your life.

The Holy Spirit, who is love, desires for you to have your heart transformed by love.

He desires to open your eyes to beauty, and also to spiritual things so that the Mass will take on special meaning for you, and the New Testament will start to come alive for you.

He desires to prompt you in what is right, and to lead you into God's special plan for your life.

All these wonderful things are important elements in Baptism in the Spirit. Jesus desires that your Confirmation become a special time of becoming open to at least some of these important blessings.

When One Is Hurt

God is love. If God's will was truly done on earth, everyone would live in peace and harmony with one another. But sin entered the world through what we call "**Original Sin**". As a result, God's plan to build a society based on love has been badly damaged.

Sometimes a child will suffer abuse from an adult. That is most painful. Jesus warned adults that it would be better for them to have a millstone tied around their neck and to be dumped into the sea, than to cause hurt to a child. But sadly it still happens.

Children can also be cruel to one another.

Bullying is one of the most serious sins a child could possibly commit, because it causes great hurt to the victim.

When one is bullied or abused, one ends up feeling isolated and inferior as a result of being hurt at the centre of one's being. One also becomes very caught up in one's own inner feelings. Instead of being confident and outgoing, one becomes nervous and turned in on oneself.

Even when the bullying or abuse stops or when one gets away from it, it can take a long time for one's inner self to heal.

Our hearts are designed by God for love; to love and to be loved. Bullying is the very opposite to love.

Being bullied also causes hurt and anger to build up in the victim's heart. God totally understands us when this happens. He desires to embrace us in His love and to heal our hurt. But until that happens, the hurt and anger in one's heart, makes it more difficult for one to love.

The bullying may have left one feeling no good and feeling inferior to others. Then one feels a need to prove oneself. One feels a need to get on better than others. God totally understand this, but it can cause us to be less than loving in the way we take part in games or other events. One has a need to impress, to do well. That can take over one's life.

Bullying can also leave one feeling very empty and very lonely. One's heart has been deprived of love.

There is only one thing that really takes away this type of inner emptiness and that is to have Jesus come alive in one's heart.

Becoming famous may give one a boost, but it cannot take away the inner emptiness.

Getting rich may give one something to aim at, and it may allow one to do fun things, but it cannot take away the inner emptiness.

Falling in love may help in the short term, but if one doesn't come to a living relationship with Jesus, the inner emptiness will eventually come back and may also destroy one's marriage.

When one's heart is empty, Jesus and Jesus alone can fill it.

Would you drive a nail into the hand of Jesus? I'm sure not.

But when we bully or abuse others, we are hurting them in their heart - in the very place that Jesus is living within them

That is what Jesus meant when He said, **"I am the bread of Life."** He once met a very sad woman by the well in Samaria. She felt very empty in heart. Jesus told her, **"He or she who drinks of the water that I shall give will never thirst again"** John 4:14. He was telling her that He was the only one who could take away the emptiness that was in her heart.

Turning to drink or to drugs to ease the pain in one's heart is an absolute disaster.

It will also lead to one becoming very very selfish, and to doing further damage to one's inner self. The only thing that the alcoholic can think of is drink. The only thing that the drug addict can think of is the next fix. They become incapable of thinking of others. They hurt their families badly. They waste their money. Drug addicts turn to stealing.

With both the drug addict and the alcoholic, their heart, which was designed for love, gets badly destroyed. All it can think about is the drink or the drugs. Only by God's power can it be healed and enabled to love again.

Jesus Gives Us Himself

Jesus desires to live in our hearts; that is in the special place deep within us where our eternal spirit is conjoined to our body. Here Jesus desires to live. It truly is the most wonderful thing that can happen in your life to have an experience of Jesus coming alive in your heart.

Jesus knew that some people would have difficulty in understanding how He could live in their hearts, so He decided to give us a very practical way of receiving Him. He did this by turning bread and wine into His body and blood at the Last Supper, and then by giving his followers the power to do the same.

During Mass, the priest takes the bread and wine, and then, speaking for Jesus, says,

> "This is my body ....
> This is my blood ....."

The priest says the words. It is Jesus who supplies the power

When we receive Holy Communion, we receive the risen Jesus.

Again Jesus knew that some people would find it very hard to believe that bread and wine could be turned into His body and blood, so while he was on earth, He showed that He had the power to change substances. **At a wedding feast in Cana, He turned water into wine.** Another time, Jesus fed up to ten thousand people **with just five loaves and two fish.**

His close friends, who had seen him turning the water into wine, and then saw him feed about ten thousand people with five small loaves and two fish, knew that Jesus had power to do extraordinary things.

So when He told them that He was going to turn water and wine into his body and blood, they believed Him.

His close friends today also believe this. They know that He loves them and that He lives in their hearts, and that He has the power to do the most amazing things. But there are many people who find this hard to believe. Jesus understands that. Just as while on earth, He performed some great miracles to help people believe, He does the same today. I have a very good friend called **Sr. Briege McKenna**. When she was only a teenager, Sr Briege got severe arthritis. By the time she was twenty two, she was crippled with it.

One day she was praying before the Sacred Host exposed on the altar.

This is what we call **Exposition of the Blessed Sacrament.** See photo across.

Looking up at Jesus in the Sacred Host, she said, **"Jesus, I'm going to find You whatever it takes."**

Shortly afterwards, at a Prayer Meeting, she heard a priest talking of the power of Jesus, and decided to ask him to pray with her at the end of the meeting. But just then she heard Jesus say to her, **"Don't look at him, look at Me."**

She closed her eyes, and said **"Jesus, please, please help me."** She felt a hand touch her head. Thinking that the priest had come down to her, she opened her eyes, but there was no one there. Feeling a sensation going through her body, she looked down at her hands and feet. Her fingers that had been all stiff with the arthritis were now fully loose. The sores on her elbows had completely disappeared. Her feet that had been deformed with the arthritis were now perfect.

Forgetting that there were people all around her, she just jumped up, screaming, **"Jesus! You're right here!"**

It is now a full forty years since that special night. Sr. Briege has remained totally free of arthritis ever since.

The following year, at Pentecost, Sr. Briege was praying before Jesus in the tabernacle, and heard Jesus say to her, **"You have my gift of healing. Go and use it."**

Soon Jesus was doing very special things through Sr. Briege. Several people were healed when she prayed with them. But very soon, Jesus also showed her, that if she was to continue to do mighty things in His name, she would need to spend a full three hours with Him in prayer each day. While many remarkable healings have occurred when Sr. Briege prays for healing, she is deeply aware that Jesus is the true healer, and that He is truly present in the Sacred Host.

Jesus has asked her to spend the three hours with Him each day, so that when she prays with people, He is truly living in her heart and the Holy Spirit can give her mental pictures of how He desires to bless people.

We too need to spend time with Jesus in prayer.

Sometimes we think that God asks us to pray to keep Him happy. But God is perfectly happy. He desires to share His happiness with us.

Jesus knows that there will always be something missing in our lives if He is not living in our hearts.

He knows that we will risk becoming selfish and causing hurt both to ourselves and to others if His love is not being poured into our hearts.

He also knows that we won't find His special plan for our lives unless we are being guided by the Holy Spirit.

Jesus sometimes spent the entire night in prayer.

Before his public mission, He spent forty days praying and fasting.

That is why He asks us to pray.

Jesus desires to bless us. He desires to come alive in our hearts and to start giving us inner strength. He desires for us to come to know Him as our best Friend. He desires to guide us into His special plan for our lives.

At first, sitting down to pray is hard. Most people feel an urge to go do something else instead. So praying does not come easy at first. But if we persevere, Jesus can really bless us through it.

Jesus also asks us to come to Mass each Sunday. If we really love Him, then we will do so. When we miss Mass on Sunday through our own fault, we are saying 'No' to Jesus and, at least in part, closing our heart to Him. This is why it is a sin to miss Mass through one's own fault. Jesus still loves us, but we are being selfish in our relationship with Him.

Receiving Jesus

One night Sr Briege McKenna received a phone call from a young priest. He had just been told that he had cancer of the throat and that his voice box would have to be removed. He had been told that he would never be able to talk again after the operation.

Worse still, he was told that he would almost certainly die in about two years. Naturally he was very upset. Because he had heard that Sr. Briege McKenna has a special gift of healing, he phoned her.

Sr. Briege often gets mental pictures or visions of what Jesus wishes to do in a person's life. It is a little like being able to watch movies in one's head.

As she started to pray with this young priest over the phone, first she had a mental picture of the woman who was healed when she touched the hem of the garment of Jesus.

On that occasion there were hundreds of people all around Jesus, pushing in on top of Him. Amongst them, there was this one woman who had been sick for twelve years. She had spent all her money going to doctors, but none of them were able to cure her.

But now, as she looked at Jesus and heard Him speak, she was suddenly filled with faith to believe that, if she could only touch the hem of His garment, she would be healed.

So she reached in, touched the hem of his garment, and a power went out from Him that went right through her and healed her instantly.

As Sr. Briege prayed with the young priest, she saw in her mind's eye this woman being healed as she touched the hem of the garment of Jesus. Then the scene changed. **She now started to have a mental picture of the priest receiving Holy Communion, and of his throat being healed as the Sacred Host went down through it.**

She now knew that this was what Jesus wished to do. So she said to the priest, "Remember the woman who was healed when she touched the hem of the garment of Jesus. Tomorrow during Mass, you will have an even greater privilege. You will be receiving Jesus in Holy Communion.

"When the Sacred Host is in your mouth and going down through your throat, ask Jesus to heal you."

Sr. Briege didn't know that this priest had lost faith in the real presence of Jesus in the Sacred Host. He no longer believed that Jesus was truly present in the Host.

For most priests, celebrating Mass is truly the high point of their day. They love to celebrate Mass every day.

But this priest only celebrated Mass when he had to do so. He hadn't planned to celebrate Mass the next day. After Sr. Briege spoke to him, however, he asked some of his friends to join him the next morning for Mass, and was completely cured during it.

Naturally after that, he really knew that Jesus is truly present in the Sacred Host, and until his death in a car accident some years later, he was rushing around telling everyone, **"Jesus is really present in the Sacred Host. When you receive Holy Communion, you really receive Jesus."**

We too need to remind ourselves that it really is Jesus we receive in Holy Communion.

There was one occasion when Jesus was trying to explain to people how He planned to give them His body and blood in Holy Communion. He told them, "Unless you eat the flesh of the son of Man and drink His blood, you cannot have life in you." (John 6:53).

His closest followers believed what He was saying, but the great crowd of people thought that He was talking nonsense and walked away.

Had Jesus only been talking symbolically, He would surely have called the people back and explained this to them. But He let them go.

This is clear proof that Jesus really meant what He said when He said, "This is my body ... This is my blood."

The Selfish Man

There was once a selfish rich man who only thought of himself. A poor man called Lazarus asked for help, but the rich man didn't help him. Lazarus died young due to being malnourished and to sleeping rough.

When Lazarus died, he found himself experiencing love the likes of which he had never experienced before. The love just filled his entire being.

Nobody had ever loved Lazarus while he was on earth.

He was dirty and he smelled. He had made some bad choices in life. Deep down, he felt really bad about these bad choices. You could say that he hated himself. He felt that he was no good.

But now, after his death, he could feel a mighty energy force of love pulsating through his inner self. It just lifted him up. He had never experienced anything remotely like it before.

As he was lifted up in this mighty Love that was in reality the Holy Spirit, he was able to look back on his life on earth. He saw all the bad things that had happened to himself.

He also saw the mistakes he had made, but the Holy Spirit helped him to see that they weren't fully his fault; that because of the way he had been hurt by the bad things that had happened to him, it had been very hard for him to make good choices.

This poor man has just received help paid for with money raised by Irish schoolchildren.

When he died, he wasn't yet fully ready for Heaven. He still had to learn to love and to be freed of his addictions. **So he spent a short period in the upper regions of Purgatory. This is where people are prepared for entry to Heaven.** Here he learned to open His heart to God's love, and he kept asking God to bless and to help the people he had let down in life - and also to bless and to help the people who had in any way helped him. Before long he was ready to join the saints in Heaven.

Later on the rich man died. People had looked up to him here on earth.

He had a big mansion and owned millions. Wherever he went, he was treated with great respect. But when he died, all that changed. He suddenly found himself in a very dark place, down in the very depths of Purgatory, at the very entrance to Hell itself.

He had always been respected, yet nobody respected him here. There was nothing here but darkness and desolation. He could feel himself being dragged even further down, and knew that further down was Hell.

He started shouting and screaming, **"I don't belong here. Somebody get me out of here."** For quite some time he struggled in fear and terror, screaming and shouting.

Then way up above he started to see a tiny chink of light. He was in complete darkness, but he could see this pinpoint of light way up above. Sensing that in some way God was in the light, he started shouting, "I'm a believer. I shouldn't be here."

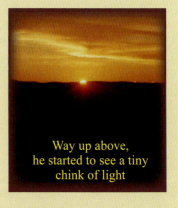

Way up above, he started to see a tiny chink of light

A great booming voice came back, "If you are a believer, what are the commandments?"

That booming voice went through him, but it also brought a bit of relief as he had always been able to answer questions about his religion.

"You shall love the Lord your God and you shall love your neighbour" he shouted back.

The great booming voice came again, "But have you loved them?"

He tried to answer 'Yes', but the echo of the great booming voice kept going right through him. Then he stuttered, "It wasn't my fault." He kept stuttering this over and over, but he could still hear the echo of the great booming voice asking "But have you loved them?"

Even as he was still stuttering "It wasn't my fault," he knew that this answer wasn't good enough, and yet it was as if he couldn't stop repeating it.

During his life on earth, he had been so attached to his wealth, and so blind to the needs of Lazarus and of the other suffering people, that he now found it really hard to accept that he was wrong. But after ages and ages in this dark place, he began to see the truth. As he did so, the light above became brighter, and he could see Abraham and Lazarus up in the presence of Jesus.

He started to cry out, "Father Abraham, please send Lazarus to help me."

But Abraham gently explained to him that this wasn't possible.

"Then please send Lazarus to warn my brothers so that they won't come to this place of torment also."

"They have the teaching of Jesus," Abraham replied. "Let them listen to Him."

In asking for help for his brothers, the rich man had at last begun to think of someone other than himself. This is part of what souls learn to do in Purgatory. They learn to think of others and to pray for others.

The rich man still had a long journey to make before he would be ready for Heaven, but at last he was beginning to move in the right direction.

He was now beginning to see how selfish he had been while on earth. As he made his millions, he had just thought of how he could have big houses and fancy cars, and how he could enjoy himself. It had never struck him that he should use his surplus wealth to help the poor. And it wasn't just Lazarus that he had neglected. There had been countless other suffering people, some even dying from starvation, yet when he had extra money, all he had thought about was how he could extend his mansion, have fancy cars and swanky clothes, and enjoy himself.

Now he could see that none of these things mattered. The only thing that mattered when one leaves one's body is how much love there is within one's eternal spirit.

He wished now that He had learned to love while on earth, but he was very thankful that God was giving him the chance to do so in Purgatory. He knew that he didn't deserve it.

Footnote:- This adaptation of the story of the rich man and Lazarus is based on the real experiences of people who had "near death experiences" as told in my book, **"I want to go to Heaven the moment I die."**

When Facing Problems

When Barbara Harris Whitfield was a little girl, her mother was continuously going into hospitals for operations. So little Barbara started praying real hard for God to send a doctor who could cure her mother. "Dear God, please send a doctor who will cure Mammy" was her number one prayer. But there was no sign of her prayer being answered.

Eventually it was easier for Barbara to believe that there is no God than to believe that there is a God but that He wasn't answering her prayers.

Many years later, when Barbara had her near death experiences, God allowed her to see that her mother had never wanted to be healed. Her mother craved attention, and her way of getting attention was by being sick and having operations.

There are many reasons why prayer may appear not be answered.

1

Every person in this life has to face suffering. The people we love die. Accidents happen. We get sick. That is the way things are. **Learning to cope with suffering is part of what we have to learn in this life.**

We don't understand why there is so much suffering, but when we learn, with God's help, to cope with suffering, our eternal spirit within us becomes stronger and more open to God's love.

2

Much suffering is brought about by people's wrong choices. Selfish people often bring hurt into the lives of those around them.

If someone is behaving in a way that is selfish, it can take much prayer to lead to their conversion. This is because God will not take away their free will. Our prayers for them can lead to God giving them special opportunities like inspiring someone to go speak to them, or to God giving them warnings, like for example inspiring their doctor to tell them that there are serious health risks arising from the lifestyle. However while God may give them several special chances or warnings, they can choose not to listen.

3

God is pure spirit. The way He normally enters our world is through human hearts - that is through Jesus coming alive in our eternal spirit within us. **The more open we are to Him, the more He can do through us.** That is why some of the saints were able to perform great miracles. They were so open to Jesus in their eternal spirit, that His power could enter the world through them, healing the sick and even raising the dead.

Sometimes we are just not open enough to God for Him to do all the things in our lives that He would love to do.

For some of the blessings that God desires to bring into the world, it would require many people to be truly open to Him living in their hearts.

Bad Things Happen To Good People

When something bad happens, people often say "It is the will of God", but it may not be God's will at all.

For example, it most certainly is not God's will that anyone drive a car while drunk, so it most certainly is not God's will if someone is killed by a drunken driver.

Many things happen that are not God's will.

Some people make selfish choices and cause hurt to others. Others live in a way that is not healthy; eat and drink in a way that is not healthy; and place themselves under stress instead of learning to trust God. If this leads to sickness, they should not blame God.

Even the air we breathe and the food we eat is often contaminated due to the wrong choices that people have made. Much illness is caused by these factors.

Sometimes wrong choices were made by our parents, or our grandparents, of even further back amongst our ancestors and so a tendency towards a particular illness may have come down through our genes and bloodlines.

This could also arise due to factors beyond our ancestors's control as many of them lived very tough lives and were very badly treated.

We also live in an imperfect world. For example, God does not will earthquakes, but yet somehow they happen.

Part of the challenge in this world is learning to overcome bad things with the help of Jesus.

In doing so, we grow stronger in our eternal spirit. The Bible promises that God works all things for the good for those who love Him. **God desires to bring blessing for you out of every bad thing that ever has happened to you or ever will happen to you.**

God Has A Plan For You

God does have a plan for your life. He desires to bless you and to bring blessing into the world through you.

When bad things happen to you, they may interfere with the externals of God's plan for your life. But no matter what happens, nobody can block God's workings in your life, so long as you walk with Him.

When bad things happen, Jesus can best help you if you take the following steps.

1. Keep inviting Jesus to live in your heart.
2. Keep reminding ourselves that God is bigger than whatever problem you face.
3. Keep reminding yourself to trust Jesus. Look at an image of the merciful Jesus and pray, **"Jesus, I trust in You."**
4. Keep bringing the hurt and anger in your heart to Jesus. Confess it in Confession. Even while still hurt and angry, follow the instruction of Jesus to "Pray for those who persecute you".
5. Remind yourself that God does have a plan for your life, and keep trusting that somehow He will work this problem for your long term good.

Follow these steps and God will bless you in mighty ways.